Peace of
Mind®

Peace of Mind
Flex Curriculum

Grades 5-8

Fifteen engaging, flexible and experiential lessons that equip students with the skills to manage big emotions, learn empathy and compassion, build healthy relationships, and express emotions in American Sign Language.

Linda Ryden and Ashley Brown
Including original stories, illustrations and videos by Linda Ryden

Welcome to the Peace of Mind Community!

Questions? Comments?
We'd love to hear from you!

Please visit teachpeaceofmind.org or
contact us at info@TeachPeaceofMind.org.

Peace of Mind Publications

Curriculum

Peace of Mind Core Curriculum for Early Childhood
Peace of Mind Core Curriculum for Grades 1 & 2
Peace of Mind Core Curriculum for Grade 3
Peace of Mind Core Curriculum for Grades 4 & 5
Peace of Mind Core Curriculum for Middle School
Peace of Mind Flex Curriculum for Kindergarten
Peace of Mind Flex Curriculum for Grades 1 & 2
Peace of Mind Flex Curriculum for Grade 3
Peace of Mind Flex Curriculum for Grade 4
Peace of Mind Flex Curriculum for Grades 5-8
Social Justice Lesson Curriculum for Grades 3-5

Storybooks

Henry is Kind
Rosie's Brain / El Cerebro de Rosita
Marleigh is Mindful / Marleigh practica la conciencia plena
Marleigh's Big Feelings
Mason and the Conflict CAT / Mason y el conflicto CAT
Quinn and the Worry Channel
Sergio Sees the Good
Tyaja Uses the Think Test

TeachPeaceofMind.org

Peace of Mind Inc. Washington DC 20015
https://TeachPeaceofMind.org
Copyright 2025 Linda Ryden and Peace of Mind Inc.

Editor: Cheryl Cole Dodwell
Cover and Interior Design: Schwa Design Group
Illustrations, Graphics and Videos: Linda Ryden
Logo: Pittny Creative
ISBN: 979-8-9998662-3-3
LCCN: 2025917682
Published 2025

Peace of Mind Flex Curriculum For Grade

Peace of Mind Flex At-a-Glance

Lesson	Topic	Mindfulness Practice and ASL	Materials Needed
		All lessons require a way to show a short video to the class and your Kindness Pal list. Worksheets and Coloring Sheets are included with the lessons.	
1.	Introduction to Peace of Mind/ Community Agreements/Peace Partners	No mindfulness in first lesson Intro ASL: Happy	1. Intro to Peace of Mind Video 2. Intro to Peace Partners Video 3. Chart paper or white board to list Community Agreements
2	Identity Maps	No mindfulness in this lesson ASL: Sad	1. Identity Maps Video 2. Sheet of paper, marker for everyone, sticky notes
3	Introduction to Mindfulness	See, Hear, Feel (in intro to mindfulness video) ASL: Scared	What is Mindfulness Video
4	Anger (introduce Mindful Leader role)	Blooming Breaths with Alexis ASL: Angry	1. Blooming Breaths Video 2. Let's Talk About Anger Video
5	Meet Your Brain	Take Five with Charles ASL: Embarrassed	1. Meet Your Brain Video 2. Take 5 Breathing with Charles
6	Apologizing	Take Five with Nick ASL: Surprised	1. Take Five with Nick Video 2. How to Apologize
7	The Conflict Escalator	Gravity Hands with Sam ASL: I Feel	1. Gravity Hands with Sam 2. The Conflict Escalator
8	The Conflict CAT	Gravity Hands with Andrew ASL: Frustrated	1. Gravity Hands 2. The Conflict CAT: Learning How to Work Out Conflicts Peacefully
9	Conflict Role Plays	Four Square Breathing ASL: Excited	Four Square Breathing with Ash
10	Metacognition	Mindful Leader Choice Remote Control Breathing (in Metacognition video) ASL: How are you feeling today?	What is Metacognition?
11	The Negativity Bias	Gratitude practice in Negativity Bias video ASL: Hungry	1. Negativity Bias video 2. Paper cups, marbles (or pasta or paperclips, something small)
12	The THiNK Test	Slow Breaths with Rose ASL: Thirsty	1. Slow Breaths with Rose 2. the THiNK Test
13	The THINK Test 2	Mindful Leader Choice ASL: Peaceful	THiNK Test Activity video
14	Just Like Me	Heartfulness and Just Like Me ASL: Worried	Just Like Me Video
15	Mindful Snowstorm	Variety ASL: Loved	No videos 1. Strips of scrap paper and pencils for everyone

Introduction to the Peace of Mind Peace of Mind Flex Curriculum

Welcome to the Peace of Mind Flex Curriculum for Grades 5-8! Through this series of fifteen flexible lessons, students will gain a better understanding of their emotions, how their brains work, and how to work out conflicts peacefully. Mindfulness, brain science, apologizing, and practical conflict resolution skills are taught as the foundation for effective conflict resolution. Each component is taught separately and then put together with Peace of Mind's Conflict CAT, an effective mindfulness-based conflict resolution method. Along the way, students will learn about the power of gratitude practice especially in moderating the brain's negativity bias; build a classroom community; enjoy getting to know their Peace Partners through discussion and activities, explore their feelings and learn how to express them in American Sign Language.

This Flex Curriculum is designed to be flexible and used in schools and out-of-school time programs where time or staffing constraints allow only 15-20 minutes for social and emotional learning practice. Lessons may be broken up into modules and taught over the course of a week.

Lessons feature mindfulness videos created by graduates of the Peace of Mind program, teaching videos and graphics by Peace of Mind founder Linda Ryden, discussion prompts, and extension activities.

Curriculum Theory of Change

Our Theory of Change (ToC) is the same for both our Flex Curriculum and our Core Curriculum. The ToC includes our Curriculum Pillars, Learning Experiences, Core Teaching Practices, and the Outcomes we hope to see for students. Here it is:

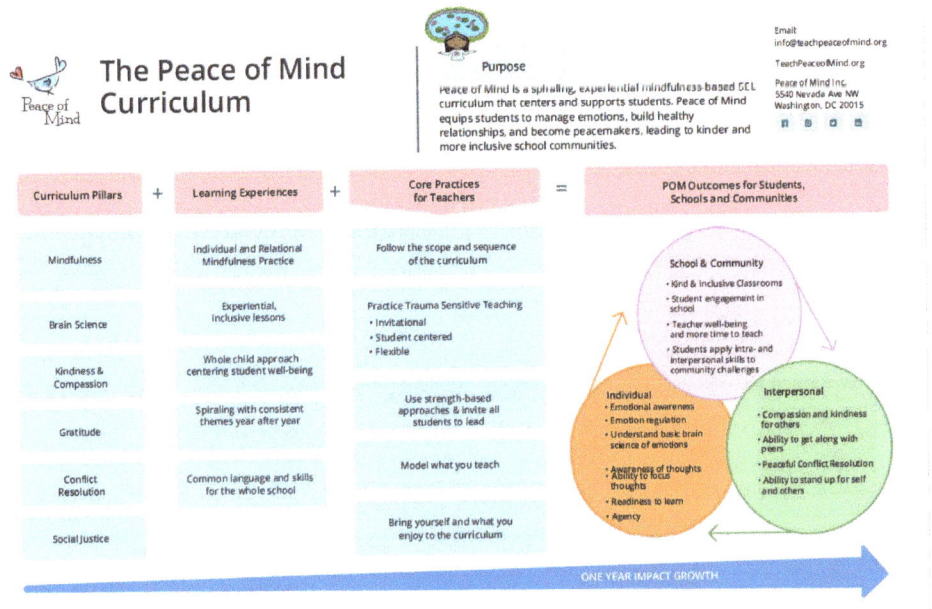

Pillars

The Peace of Mind Flex Curriculum is built on Peace of Mind's 6 foundational pillars: Mindfulness, Brain Science, Kindness and Compassion, Gratitude, Conflict Resolution and Social Justice. Engaging and fun, this Flex Curriculum features original video-based lessons and mindfulness practice videos along with interactive discussions and activities to engage students in mindfulness practice and learn what happens in their brains when they experience a big emotion and how mindful practices can affect their ability to respond. Each lesson contains a new feelings word in ASL and an opportunity for a Feelings Check-In using ASL. Every lesson ends with Peace Partners, a pair practice that helps kids get to know each other and build a caring classroom community in a relatively short time.

Former U.S. Surgeon General Vivek Murthy said that "mental health is the defining public health crisis of our time." The ultimate goal of the Peace of Mind Program is to create a kinder, more peaceful world with and for our children. We begin by helping to create classroom communities where students feel loved and seen. We help children, teens and their grownups learn how to recognize and manage their emotions, how to feel compassion for others and themselves and how to work out conflicts peacefully. We hope that with these personal and interpersonal skills, young people will grow up to find peaceful solutions to the most challenging social justice issues of our time.

Outcomes

When taught with fidelity, the Flex Curriculum will help students to:
- increase their self-awareness and self-regulation;
- understand the basic science related to their emotions;
- regularly practice kindness, compassion and gratitude;
- be more aware of and more skillfully focus their thoughts;
- build positive relationships with peers and adults;
- build kind and inclusive classrooms;
- learn how to resolve conflicts peacefully and skillfully;
- learn how to recognize, name and express their emotions in ASL.

Core Teaching Practices

Through our work with partner schools and programs as well as academic researchers, we have identified five core practices for effective, impactful implementation of Peace of Mind.

1. Follow the Scope and Sequence of the Curriculum

The curriculum's lesson sequence is designed to give students a foundational set of mindfulness practices to help them manage their emotions and learn to put space between their reactions to a big feeling and their response. We then build on that foundation adding brain

science - both an introduction to what happens in your brain when you feel big emotions and also the brain's tendency to focus on and remember negative things more than positive things - the Negativity Bias. Gratitude practice helps us to hack our Negativity Bias. Then we learn about mindful communication through the THiNK Test and a lesson about Apologizing. Finally we learn about conflict and learn and practice the Peace of Mind conflict resolution method The Conflict CAT. The curriculum, like every lesson, ends with kindness practice.

2. **Practice Trauma Sensitive Teaching**

   All lessons include three important components of trauma-sensitive teaching in the lesson scripts:

   - **Invitational** - Mindfulness practice is always invitational. While we expect everyone to sit together during the mindful moments, we invite students to choose whether or not to engage with a practice. They can choose for themselves, but they cannot interfere with someone else's choice, so we ask everyone to be respectful of others while making their own decision about whether to do a practice or not. Students are welcome to just sit quietly.

   - **Student-centered** - We teach mindfulness practices for students' own well-being. We teach a variety of practices not so students can master them all, but so they can find the ones that work best for them. If a student is having a hard time with a practice, suggest that they choose another one that works better for them.

   - **Flexible** - we don't require students to close their eyes or sit in a certain way to practice. If students need to make modifications to a practice (keeping their eyes open or walking quietly in the back of the room, for example) to help themselves feel comfortable, this is fine as long as their choices do not interfere with others' comfort and safety.

3. **Use Strength-Based Approaches**

   You will notice that the scripts offered for the lessons use strength-based language that focuses on students' abilities, interests and potential, not deficits.

   The curriculum is designed to promote student agency and leadership, especially through the role of Mindful Leader. The Mindful Leader is a student who leads the class in the mindfulness practice for the day. Here's how it works:

   - The teacher consults their class list and chooses a student to be the Mindful Leader (ML) for the day.

- The teacher encourages the class to offer sign language applause for the person who is chosen that day.

- The ML comes to the front of the class and sits next to the teacher on a chair or on the floor if you are sitting in a circle.

- With the teacher's help the ML says slowly, "Let's get into our mindful bodies…. Let's close our eyes or look down. … Let's take three deep breaths." Always offer the students a choice about keeping their eyes open or closed.

- At this point the teacher will lead the rest of the mindfulness practice as instructed in the lesson.

- The ML rings the bell/chime when the mindfulness practice is complete.

- The teacher then asks the ML to return to their seat.

You may need to help students remember what to say at the beginning of the year. Repeating the same words each class is important to help students develop a routine to help them begin to practice on their own.

4. Model What you Teach

We know from research and our own experience that modeling what we are teaching is one of the most effective ways of engaging our students in mindfulness practice themselves. Students will take their cues from you. You don't have to be an expert in mindfulness but it is very helpful to model using mindful practices yourself.

5. Bring Yourself to the Curriculum

Once you are comfortable with the first four core practices, we hope you will be able to bring yourself to the curriculum. If the script isn't quite how you would say things, please adapt so you feel comfortable!

Setting Expectations

The **Peace of Mind** curriculum is planting seeds of mindfulness and compassion. These seeds grow and mature inside a student's mind and heart, positively affecting the way a person sees the world and operates within it. For some students, the outward positive effects are manifested quickly and clearly. For other students, it may take more time, and the outward signs of change may be subtle. All that we expect of students is to try to practice the skills in this curriculum as often as they can. Just to try.

Some kids have a much easier time sitting quietly than others. Keep your expectations reasonable. Sometimes the kid who is sitting with eyes wide open, legs jiggling, and fiddling with a pencil—but not talking—during mindfulness

practice is doing their very best and is benefiting greatly from the effort. That's okay. The exercises in this curriculum are for the benefit of the students and, as long as they are not preventing others from practicing, a little wiggling around is okay.

Try to put the guidelines in positive language such as "As long as you follow the directions you can continue to play the game." This can be much more effective than the more traditional way of saying, "If you don't follow the rules you can't play." Many students react defiantly to orders like that but are perfectly happy to follow the rules when they are stated in a more neutral way.

Materials Needed

- A bell or a chime

- A means to play videos for the class

- Slide Deck for the Flex Curricula for Grades 5-8. Accessible through QR code here:

American Sign Language

A new addition to the Peace of Mind Curriculum, American Sign Language is a wonderful tool to use to help all children, regardless of English proficiency, learn about, explore and communicate their emotions. These lessons offer a very basic, simple introduction to expressing emotions in American Sign Language. The ASL included in these lessons is just an introduction to a rich language that can be used to communicate with students who are deaf and hard of hearing or who have other communication challenges.

For more information about learning ASL please visit: www.nad.org/resources/american-sign-language/learning-american-sign-language

A Note on Peace Partners

Peace Partners is an engaging and powerful activity that takes place every class period. Here is a quick video introduction to the concept and how it works. You'll show this video in Lesson 1. Peace Partner practice reminds young people to make kindness part of their daily lives. Doing kind things for their Peace Partners spills over into their treatment of others, helping students develop the habit of treating people with kindness through regular practice. Peace Partners also gives students opportunities to get to know each other and to connect with others whom they might not have gotten along with in the past or whom they think they just don't like. Here is how it works:

- Each class you assign each student one Peace Partner. You can pair them up in advance to ensure there aren't any repeats.

- When they receive the names of their Peace Partners, emphasize that both students, or the whole class, must say "Okay." This is very important. This lets the teacher know that they have heard their assignment and that they know who their Peace Partners are. Please practice this with your class.

- Please let the class know that this is not a time for them to let the teacher or the class know how they feel about having that Peace Partner. This avoids hurt feelings and also offers multiple chances to remind the students that they have the power to be kind and the power to hurt people's feelings. It all depends on their choices. This is a powerful lesson.

- Explain to the students that they will each receive one Peace Partner each class period (or each week if you choose). Peace Partners will participate in an activity together during the class period.

- You may also invite the students to do small kind things for their assigned Peace Partners before the next class. The following class, allow a few minutes for them to talk about what they did for their Partner.

- Assign new Partners each time the class meets. If you have an odd number of students you can ask somebody to volunteer to have two Peace Partners and they can work together as a trio.

Lesson 1
Welcome to Peace of Mind!

Slides: 1-12

1. Welcome to Peace of Mind!

You might say: *In this class we're going to be talking about our thoughts and emotions and we're going to be learning how to work out conflicts peacefully. Let's watch this video introduction to Peace of Mind. Watch introduction to Peace of Mind video* (1:09) (optional)

2. Create Community Agreements

You might say: *In this class we are going to be talking about our feelings, our thoughts, how we treat other people and how we treat ourselves. It's going to be important that everyone feels comfortable sharing their thoughts and it's important that it is okay for us to disagree respectfully.*

Discuss
- Can you describe a time when you felt comfortable, when you felt like you mattered, when you felt respected and safe? What made you feel that way?
- How can we make this a place where everybody feels that way?
- What should we agree to do or not to do to make this space feel like that?

You might say: *Let's brainstorm some community agreements. These aren't rules but rather things that we all agree to do or not to do so that everyone feels welcome and safe to share.*

Invite some suggestions. Encourage the students to word the agreements in positive language. "We will be kind to each other" rather than "Don't be mean."

Here are some suggestions that cover a lot of ground. Suggestion (if helpful):
- We will listen to each other.
- We will talk when it is our turn.
- We will support each other.
- We will give each other chances to do better.
- We will do our best to be kind.

Ask: How will we handle it if our agreements are broken?

Brainstorm some possibilities:

- Say "ouch" when an agreement is broken

- Let each other know as soon as you feel uncomfortable

- Stop and talk about it

- Start again

- Reframe agreements as necessary.

Write up and post the Community Agreements and refer back to them frequently.

3. American Sign Language (ASL)

You might say: *We're going to be learning a new way to share our feelings with each other called American Sign Language or ASL. ASL is a visual language - a language that we see with our eyes instead of listening to with our ears.*

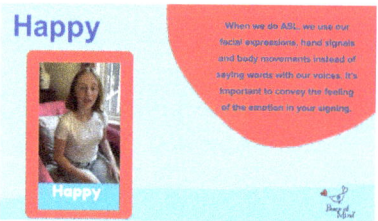

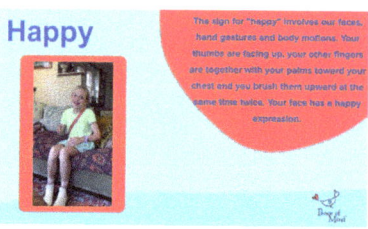

When we use ASL, we use our facial expressions, hand signals and body movements instead of saying words with our voices. Most of the people who use ASL are deaf, which means that they cannot hear with their ears, or hard of hearing which means they have trouble hearing with their ears. But lots of other people use it too. Once we learn how to share our feelings in ASL, we'll start using it to share our feelings with each other.

We're going to start out by learning how to say "happy. "
How do you feel in your body when you are happy? Take some answers.

Choose a few volunteers to demonstrate what "happy" looks like.

You might say: *Let's watch a video of one of the Peace of Mind students showing us how to sign "happy."* **(the video is in the slides and here)**

4. Icebreaker: This or That

Students walk to different sides of the room based on their preferences. They have to pick one.

- Would you rather have a dog or a cat?

- Would you rather be a dog or a cat?

- Would you rather eat french fries or potato chips?

- Would you rather eat carrots or celery?

- Would you rather be a bird or a bat?

- Would you rather live in the future or the past?

- Would you rather be able to talk to animals or speak all human languages?

- Would you rather explore space or the ocean?

- Would you rather be invisible or be able to fly?

5. Peace Partners

Introduce Peace Partners: *One of the ways that we're going to be getting to know each other, and ourselves, a little better is through Peace Partners. Let's watch this video to find out more:* **Watch** Intro to Peace Partners video - **(2:35)** (optional)

Discuss Peace Partners

- Who can tell me what the rule is for Peace Partners?

- Why do you think it's important to say "Okay!"

- Do you have to be friends with your Peace Partner?

- Can you be kind to someone who isn't already your friend?

- Can you be kind to someone you don't know very well?

- Can you think of a time that you were kind to someone that you didn't know or didn't really like?

- Are you allowed to have your feelings about who your Peace Partner is? (yes!)

- Would it be kind to let your Peace Partner (and everybody else) know that you're not feeling great about it? Can you talk to somebody else about it later like a friend, teacher or parent instead?

Assign Peace Partners (remind the kids to say "Okay!") You can make a list ahead of time, put students' names on popsicle sticks and pull them

randomly out of a jar, or however you want to do them is fine. Just make sure that they get a different partner each time.

You might say: *Okay so let's try it. I'm going to tell you who your Peace Partner is going to be. Don't forget to say "Okay!"*

Peace Partners activity: Two Truths and a Lie

You might say: *Now we're going to do an activity with your Peace Partner. When I say "Go!" you're going to find your Peace Partner and then you'll have a few minutes to play Two Truths and a Lie. You and your partner will take turns telling two truths about yourselves and one lie. Your partner has to guess what is true and what isn't true about you.*

Share: Take a moment to let them share something they learned about their Peace Partners.

6. Closing

You might say: *Let's take a moment to think about something kind you could do for your Peace Partner today. You can close your eyes if you want to.*
Wait.
Ask: *Who has an idea already of what you might do?* **Take a few answers.**
Say: *Thanks for a great class, everyone!*
Ring a bell or chime if you have one.

Lesson 2
Who Am I?

<u>*Slides: 13-21*</u>

1. Introduction

You might say: *In this lesson we're going to make Identity Maps. We'll be thinking about all of the different aspects of our identities and the roles we play. We'll use our identity maps to introduce ourselves to the group.*

2. Identity Maps

<u>**Watch Identity Map Video**</u> (3:17)

Make Identity Maps - Hand out a sheet of paper, a few sticky notes, and a marker to everyone.

Have students tear the sticky notes into thinner strips so they have several thin sticky notes.

Follow directions in the video: have students draw a circle in the middle of the paper and put their name in the middle. Around the outside, write the roles you play and what makes you "you".

The students will be sharing their identity maps during the Gallery Walk so remind them that they shouldn't include anything that they don't want to share with the class.

Gallery Walk: Have everyone put their Identity Map on the wall or leave them on their desks and do a Gallery Walk so everyone can **silently** look at the other Identity Maps. While they are walking, students can place a sticky note on another student's Identity Map when they find something they have in common. This is a good time to remind students about the class agreements and about treating each other with kindness.

Discuss:
- What did you notice that you have in common with someone else?
- Were you surprised by anything you learned about yourself or someone else?
- What are some of the most important aspects of your identity to you?

3. American Sign Language (ASL)

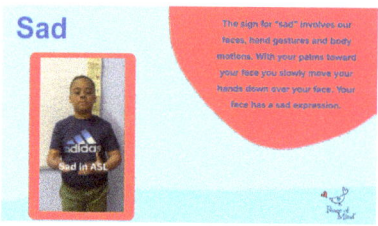

You might say: *Today we're going to learn how to say "sad" in ASL. How do you feel in your body when you are sad?*

Choose a few volunteers to demonstrate what "sad" looks like.

You might say: *Let's watch a video of one of the Peace of Mind students showing us how to sign "sad."* **(the video is in the slides and here.)**

ASL Practice

Have everyone try to say "sad" in ASL. Point out that the sign for "sad" involves our faces, hand gestures and body motions. Ask them if the sign for sad matches the way that they feel when they are sad.

4. Peace Partners

Assign Peace Partners as in Lesson 1. **Ask** someone to state the Peace Partner rule (say "Okay!") and why that's important.

Peace Partner Activity: Share Identity Maps
You might say: *Sit with your Peace Partner and share your Identity Maps. Notice what you have in common and what is different about the two of you.*

5. Closing

You might say: *Thanks for a great class, everyone! Let's take a moment to think about something kind you could do for your Peace Partner today. You can close your eyes if you want to.*
Wait.
Ask: *Who has an idea already of what you might do?* ***Take a few answers.***
Say: *Thanks for a great class, everyone!*
Ring a bell or chime if you have one.

Sample Identity Map

Lesson 3
Introduction to Mindfulness

Slides: 23-29

1. Introduction

In this lesson we introduce mindfulness. The "What is Mindfulness?" video explains what mindfulness is, why it is relevant to students' lives, and gives students a chance to practice.

2. Mindful Moment

Watch What is Mindfulness Video (5:12) - be prepared to stop the video throughout where marked, or wherever you find useful, for discussion.

Discuss:

- Have you heard of mindfulness before?
- Now that you know more about it, is it different than what you thought it was?
- Can you name any of the famous people who practice mindfulness?
- Why do you think mindfulness would be helpful for them?
- Can you think of times that mindfulness could be helpful for you?
- The practice in the video that we tried is called "See, Hear, Feel". You can try that anytime on your own. You can just close your eyes or look down and notice what you see, hear and feel.

3. American Sign Language (ASL)

You might say: *Today we're going to learn how to say "scared" in ASL. How do you feel in your body when you feel scared?*

Choose a few volunteers to demonstrate what "scared" looks like.

You might say: *Let's watch a video of one of the Peace of Mind students showing us how to sign "scared."* **(the video is in the slides and here.)**

ASL Practice

Have everyone try to say "scared" in ASL. Point out that the sign for scared involves our faces, hand gestures and body motions. Ask them if the sign for scared matches the way that they feel when they are scared.

4. Peace Partners

Assign Peace Partners as in Lesson 1. Ask someone to state the Peace Partner rule (say "Okay!") and why that's important.

Peace Partner Activity: Interview your Peace Partner

Students act as interviewers and then reporters - they can ask questions about their partner's hobbies, favorite subject, favorite ice cream, etc. They can take turns interviewing each other. They can try to remember their partner's answers or take notes.

Share

Have each student "report" something they learned about their Peace Partner to the group.

5. Closing

You might say: *Let's take a moment to think about something kind you could do for your Peace Partner today. You can close your eyes if you want to.*
Wait.
Ask: *Who has an idea already of what you might do?* **Take a few answers.**
Say: *Thanks for a great class, everyone!*
Ring a bell or chime if you have one.

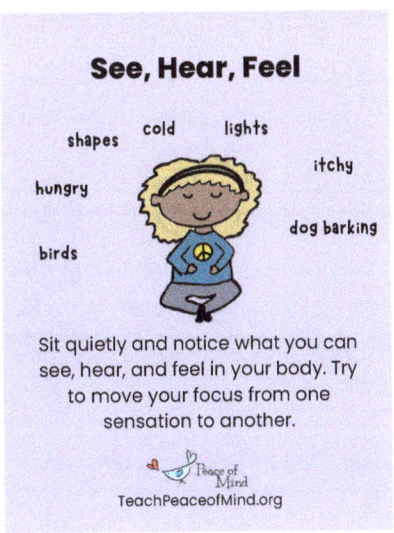

Lesson 4
Let's Talk About Anger

Slides: 30-38

1. Introduction

You might say: *Today I'm going to choose a Mindful Leader. From now on, one of you will help to lead the mindfulness practice that we'll learn in the videos. We're going to practice mindfulness by learning a practice called Blooming Breaths created by a middle school student named Alexis. She'll demonstrate it in this video. Then we're going to learn a little bit about an emotion that can sometimes be challenging: anger.*

2. Mindful Moment

Watch mindfulness video Blooming Breaths with Alexis (1:35)

Choose a Mindful Leader

You might say: *So now I'm going to choose a volunteer to help to lead the mindfulness practice called the Mindful Leader. The Mindful Leader will help to lead the mindfulness practice that we'll learn in the videos by saying:*

• Let's get into our mindful bodies.

• Let's close our eyes or look down.

• Let's take 3 deep breaths.

We'll use the same language every time so that you will get used to it and you'll be able to practice mindfulness on your own if you choose to.

Practice Blooming Breaths

With your help, have the Mindful Leader say the words above and lead the class in doing three Blooming Breaths.

3. American Sign Language (ASL)

You might say: *Today we're going to learn how to say "angry" in ASL. How do you feel in your body when you are angry?*

Choose a few volunteers to demonstrate what "angry" looks like.

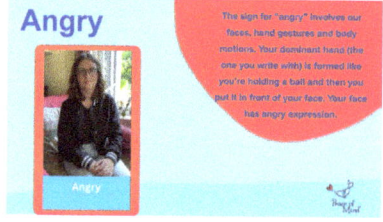

You might say: *Let's watch a video of one of the Peace of Mind students showing us how to sign "angry."* (the video is in the slides and here)

ASL Practice

Have everyone try to say "angry" in ASL. Point out that the sign for "angry" involves our faces, hand gestures and body motions. Ask them if the sign for angry matches the way that they feel when they are angry.

Watch Anger [video](#) (3:33)

You might say: *Now we're going to watch a video to learn a little bit about anger.*

Be prepared to stop the video where it says "Pause the video" and let some kids answer or discuss with a neighbor.

Discuss
- Can you think of some times when you got angry?
- How do you usually feel when you get angry?
- How do you usually express your anger?
- Do you express your anger?
- What do you do to calm yourself down when you get angry?

4. Peace Partners

Assign Peace Partners as in Lesson 1. Remind the students to say "Okay!"

Peace Partner Activity: Commonalities

Assign each Peace Partner pair another pair of Peace Partners and give them a few minutes to meet with the other pair to find out what they have in common. Then have them brainstorm ways they could be kind to the other pair.

5. Closing

You might say: *Let's take a moment to think about something kind you could do for your Peace Partner today. You can close your eyes if you want to.*
Wait.
Ask: Who has an idea already of what you might do? Take a few answers.
Say: Thanks for a great class, everyone!
Ring a bell or chime if you have one.

Lesson 5
Meet Your Brain

Slides: 39-46

1. Introduction

You might say: Today we're going to be learning about what happens in our brains when we are experiencing big emotions like anger. First, we're going to learn another mindfulness practice with a middle schooler named Charles.

2. Mindful Moment

Watch Mindfulness Video (Take Five with Charles) (0:55)

Choose the Mindful Leader

Practice Take Five Breathing. Have the Mindful Leader lead the mindfulness practice as in Lesson 4.

3. American Sign Language (ASL)

You might say: Today we're going to learn how to say "embarrassed" in ASL. How do you feel in your body when you feel embarrassed?

Choose a few volunteers to demonstrate what "embarrassed" looks like.

You might say: Let's watch a video of one of the Peace of Mind students showing us how to sign "embarrassed." **(the video is in the slides and here)**

ASL Practice

Have everyone try to say "embarrassed" in ASL. Point out that the sign involves our faces, hand gestures and body motions. Ask them if the sign matches the way that they feel when they are embarrassed.

4. Brain Science

Watch Meet Your Brain Video (7:04) Stop where it says "Pause the video" and let students answer the question prompts or discuss with a neighbor.

Discuss:

- Can you think of a time when your amygdala was protecting you?

- Can you think of a time when your amygdala overreacted?

- Can you think of a time when you got angry and your amygdala took over? Did it choose fight, flight or freeze?

You might say: *As we said in the first class we are learning about conflict resolution. Learning about mindfulness and about brain science are two of the most important things to know to help you to work out conflicts peacefully. Next time we'll learn about apologizing.*

5. Peace Partners

Assign Peace Partners as in Lesson 1.

Peace Partners Activity

You might say: *When I say "go", you and your Peace Partner are going to create a bucket list of things you want to do this year. A bucket list can be things that are really possible to do - like reading 10 books - or it could be something you dream about - like going to the moon or meeting your favorite singer.*

6. Closing

You might say: *Let's take a moment to think about something kind you could do for your Peace Partner today. You can close your eyes if you want to.*
Wait.
Ask: *Who has an idea already of what you might do?* **Take a few answers.**
Say: *Thanks for a great class, everyone!*
Ring a bell or chime if you have one.

_____

Extension: *See The Peace of Mind Core Curriculum for Middle School, Unit 4, for additional Brain Science lessons starting on page 89.*

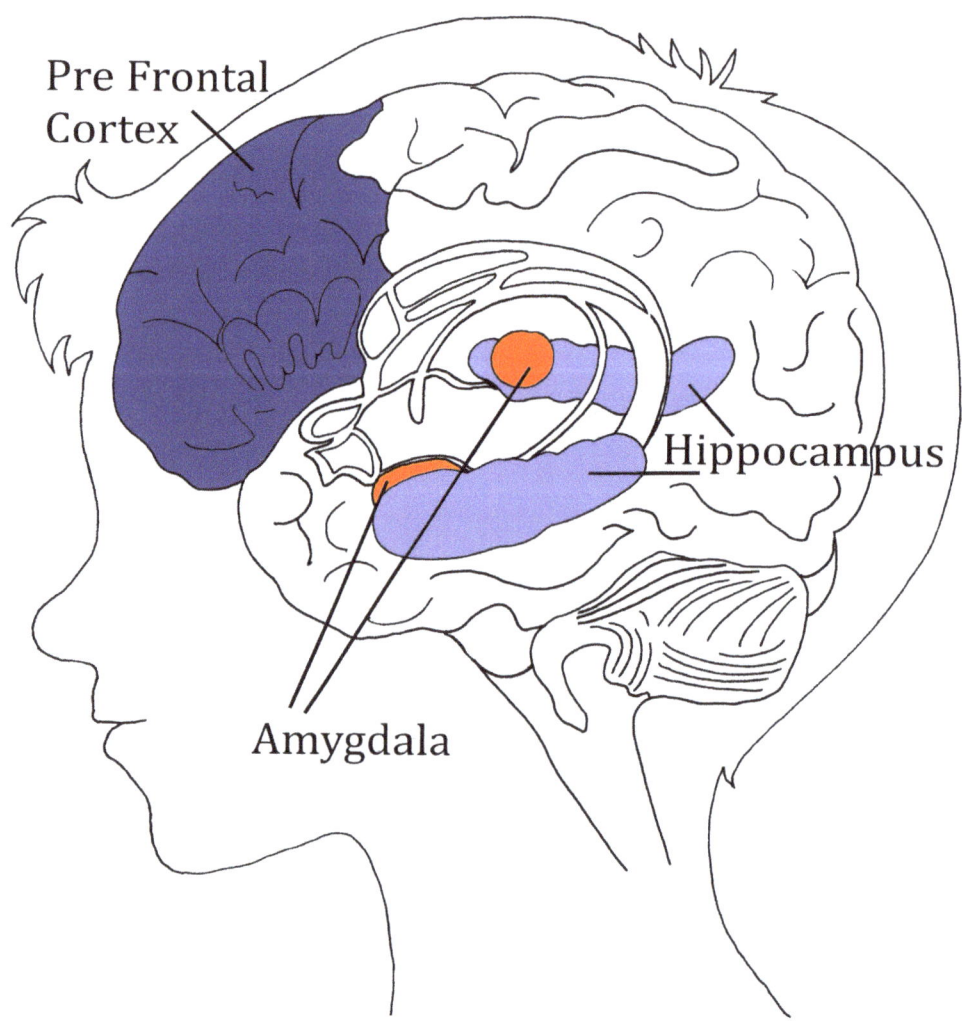

Pre Frontal Cortex

Hippocampus

Amygdala

Lesson 6
Apologizing

Slides: 47-54

1. Introduction

You might say: *Today we're going to be learning about a really important part of working out conflicts peacefully: apologizing. Today I'm going to tell you who your Peace Partner is before we watch the video about apologizing. Then whenever there are questions in the video, you are going to talk them over with your Peace Partner before answering. But first we're going to practice Take 5 breathing again with a middle schooler named Nick.*

2. Mindful Moment

Watch Mindfulness Video (Take Five with Nick) (0:59)

Choose the Mindful Leader.

Practice Take Five Breathing
Have the Mindful Leader lead the mindfulness practice - see Lesson 4 for instructions.

3. American Sign Language (ASL)

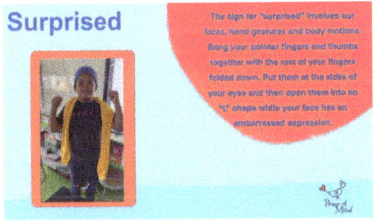

You might say: *Today we're going to learn how to say "surprised" in ASL. How do you feel in your body when you feel surprised?*

Choose a few volunteers to demonstrate what "surprised" looks like.

You might say: *Let's watch a video of one of the Peace of Mind students showing us how to sign "surprised"* **(the video is in the slides and here.)**

ASL Practice
Have everyone try to say "surprised" in ASL. Point out that the sign involves our faces, hand gestures and body motions. Ask them if the sign matches the way that they feel when they are surprised.

4. Peace Partners

Assign Peace Partners as in Lesson 1.

Peace Partners Activity: Discuss Apologizing

You might say: *There are several places in today's video where we will stop the video and you and your Peace Partner will answer the questions and discuss together for a moment.*

Watch How to Apologize Video (7:26) Stop where it says "Pause the video" and allow time for the students to confer with their Peace Partners to answer the questions.

5. Closing

You might say: *Let's take a moment to think about something kind you could do for your Peace Partner today. You can close your eyes if you want to.*

Wait.

Ask: *Who has an idea already of what you might do?* **Take a few answers.**

Say: *Thanks for a great class, everyone!*

Ring a bell or chime if you have one.

Extensions: *See the Peace of Mind Core Curriculum for Middle School Unit 5, for 5 full lessons on Conflict Resolution, including apologizing. Page 110.*

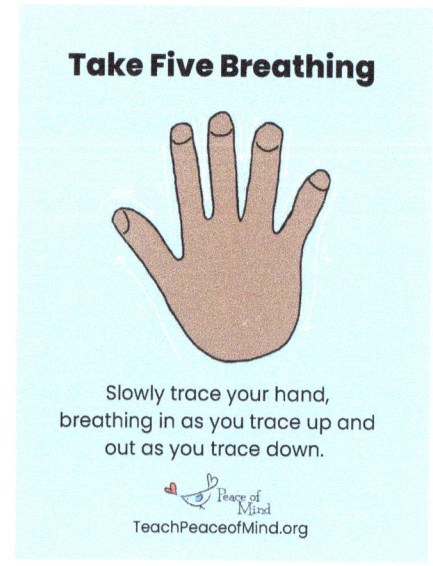

Take Five Breathing

Slowly trace your hand, breathing in as you trace up and out as you trace down.

Peace of Mind
TeachPeaceofMind.org

Lesson 7
The Conflict Escalator

Slides: 55-69

1. Introduction

You might say: *Today we're going to learn about how conflicts escalate or get bigger by learning about the Conflict Escalator. But first let's do our Mindfulness practice.*

2. Mindful Moment

Watch Mindfulness Video ([Gravity Hands with Sam](#)) (2:09)

Practice Gravity Hands.
Have the Mindful Leader lead the mindfulness practice as in Lesson 4.

3. American Sign Language (ASL)

You might say: *Today we're going to learn how to say "I feel" in ASL. Then we can start to say "I feel happy or I feel sad, etc."*

You might say: *Let's watch a video of one of the Peace of Mind students showing us how to sign "I feel."* **(the video is in the slides and [here](#))**

ASL Practice
Have everyone try to say "I feel" in ASL. Then try adding some of the feeling words you've learned so far.

4. Conflict Resolution

Watch [Conflict Escalator Video: Scrabble Vs. Monopoly Skit](#) (3:06)

Discuss:
- What was the conflict in this skit?
- What caused the conflict to escalate?
- What did the kids do to work out the conflict peacefully?
- What kinds of things do you think cause conflicts to escalate? (tone of voice, insults, etc.)

- What part of your brain do you think would be in charge if you are going up the Conflict Escalator? (Amygdala)

Do you think taking deep breaths could be helpful when you're trying to come down the Conflict Escalator?

5. Whole Group Activity: Count to Ten Game

You might say: *Today we are going to try to count to ten as a group. That sounds easy but it's actually pretty hard. The point of this game is to try to count to ten as a group, one at a time. This is how it works:*

- You'll close your eyes or look down into your lap and listen carefully.

- At some point, one of you will say "one" and then someone else will say "two," and we'll keep going until we get to ten.

- Every time I hear two of you say a number at the same time, you'll have to start all over again at one.

- To make the game work, you are going to have to listen very carefully to each other. You are also going to have to be mindful of not taking too many turns. You also have to be mindful of making sure that you participate.

- If we get to ten, we can keep going.

- To start things out, I will say, **"Let's go."** After that, every time I hear two of you say a number at the same time I will say, **"Start again and go."** We'll start again at one.

- Try not to make a lot of noise when that happens. Just take a deep breath and start over again. Ready to try it?

> *Note: This game is harder than it sounds. Encourage the students to be patient and kind with each other. There will of course be kids who want to say all the numbers who might need gentle reminders not to dominate the game, and there will also be those who will need encouragement to participate. You can start each round with a mindfulness breath to reset focus and encourage patience.*

6. Peace Partners

Assign Peace Partners as in Lesson 1.

Peace Partners Activity: Commonalities
You might say: *When I say "go" you and your Peace Partner are going to get together and see how many things you can find that you have in common in 60 seconds. Keep track of your number and we'll see who the winner is when we're done.*

7. Closing

You might say: *Let's take a moment to think about something kind you could do for your Peace Partner today. You can close your eyes if you want to.*
Wait.
Ask: *Who has an idea already of what you might do?* **Take a few answers.**
Say: *Thanks for a great class, everyone!*
Ring a bell or chime if you have one.

Extension: *See the Peace of Mind Core Curriculum for Middle School Unit 5, for 5 full lessons on Conflict Resolution, including the Conflict Escalator. Page 110.*

Gravity Hands

Slowly move your hands up and down as you breathe in and out.

Peace of Mind
TeachPeaceofMind.org

Lesson 8
The Conflict CAT

Slides: 70-78

1. Introduction

You might say: _In this class we're going to put all the pieces together to learn about working out conflicts peacefully. We've learned about mindfulness, brain science, apologizing, and how conflicts escalate. Now we'll learn what we can do to bring conflicts down the Conflict Escalator and figure out a way to work things out that will be okay for everyone involved._

2. Mindful Moment

Watch Mindfulness Video Gravity Hands with Andrew (00:49).

Practice Gravity Hands led by Mindful Leader.

3. American Sign Language (ASL)

You might say: _Today we're going to learn how to say "frustrated" in ASL. How do you feel in your body when you feel frustrated?_

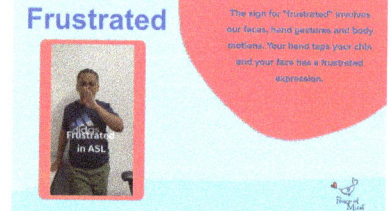

Choose a few volunteers to demonstrate what "frustrated" looks like.

You might say: _Let's watch a video of one of the Peace of Mind students showing us how to sign "frustrated."_ **(the video is in the slides and here)**

ASL Practice: Have everyone try to say "frustrated" in ASL.

4. Conflict Resolution

Watch Conflict CAT video (6:24) Stop where it says "Pause the video" and let some students answer or discuss with a neighbor.

5. Peace Partners

Assign Peace Partners as in Lesson 1.

Peace Partners Activity: Conflict CAT

You might say: *When I say "Go" you're going to find your new Peace Partner and the two of you will see if you can remember what the letters stand for in the Conflict CAT and see if you can name some of the 8 tools in the toolbox.*

6. **Whole Group Activity:** Walk, Stop, Wiggle, Sit

You might say: *Okay - let's get up and move around and do a brain challenge.*

Directions
There are many levels of this game. In each level, see if you can follow my directions. We're going to play the game silently so that everyone can hear the directions. Make sure that you are not talking and that you are not touching each other.

Level 1: *When I say walk, you walk. When I say stop, you stop. When I say wiggle, you wiggle. When I say sit, you sit. Got it?*

Level 2: Walk = Stop
Stop = Walk
Wiggle = Wiggle
Sit = Sit

Level 3: Walk = Stop
Stop = Walk
Wiggle = Sit
Sit = Wiggle

Level 4: Walk = Wiggle
Wiggle = Walk
Sit = Stop
Stop = Sit

You can keep going, changing up the commands or add in new ones. It's pretty hard!

Discuss

- What was the hardest thing about this game?

- Why do you think it is hard for our brains to "go" when someone says "stop?"

- Do you think this game is challenging to your brain?

- Did your brain get used to doing different things after a while?

6. Closing

You might say: *Let's take a moment to think about something kind you could do for your Peace Partner today. You can close your eyes if you want to.*
Wait.
Ask: *Who has an idea already of what you might do?* **Take a few answers.**
Say: *Thanks for a great class, everyone!*
Ring a bell or chime if you have one.

Extensions: *See the Peace of Mind Core Curriculum for Middle School Unit 5, for 5 full lessons on Conflict Resolution, including the Conflict CAT. Page 110.*

The Conflict C.A.T.

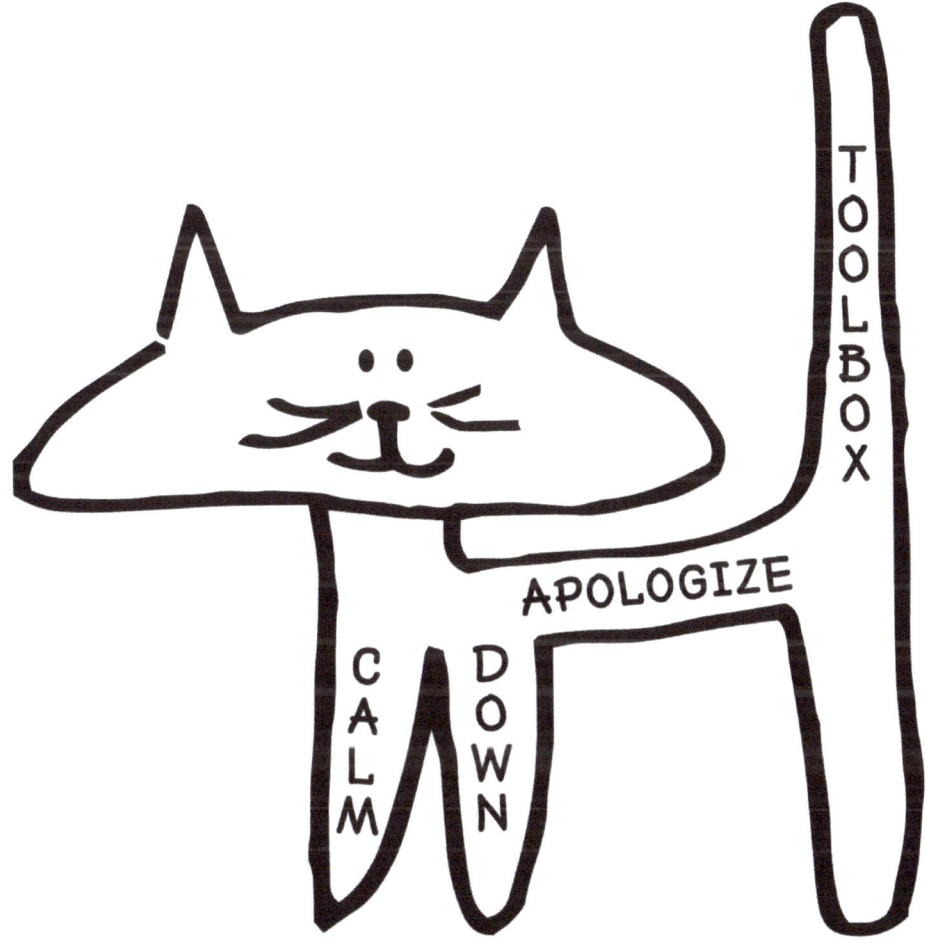

Lesson 9
Conflict Role Plays

Slides: 79-87

1. Introduction

You might say: *Today you get to practice using the Conflict CAT with your Peace Partner. But first we're going to learn another mindfulness practice with a high schooler named Ash.*

2. Mindful Moment

Watch Mindfulness Video Four Square Breathing with Ash (00:29).

Choose the Mindful Leader

Practice Four Square Breathing. Have the Mindful Leader lead the mindfulness practice as before.

3. American Sign Language (ASL)

You might say:*Today we're going to learn how to say "excited" in ASL. How do you feel in your body when you feel excited?*

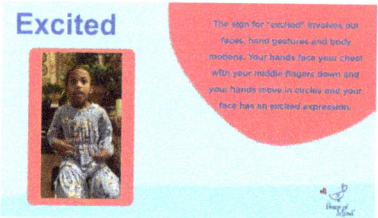

Choose a few volunteers to demonstrate what "excited" looks like.

You might say: *Let's watch a video of one of the Peace of Mind students showing us how to sign "excited."* **(the video is in the slides and here)**

ASL Practice: Have everyone try to say "excited" in ASL. Does the sign for "excited" match the way your body feels when you feel excited?

4. Conflict Resolution

Review the Conflict CAT

Choose two students to teach the Conflict CAT to the class. Be sure they include the 8 tools in the toolbox. See Anchor Chart below.

5. Peace Partners

Assign Peace Partners as in Lesson 1.

Peace Partners Activity

You might say: *We've learned a lot about working out conflicts so far. We've learned how to use breathing to help us to calm down, we've learned about our brains, we've practiced apologizing, we've learned about the Conflict Escalator, and we've learned 8 tools to use to work out conflicts. Today we're going to put it all together. I'm going to give you and your Peace Partner a conflict to work out in a role play. You'll have a few minutes to work out how you are going to do it and which tool you are going to use.*

> **Note:** *Some students might question the idea of using language like "We're going up the Conflict Escalator!" They might say that the language is corny or ridiculous. Reassure them that that is the idea. We are hoping that the language - while important and useful - does sound funny and that when we find things funny and laugh about them it can be easier to remember them. We realize that this isn't how they are going to talk when they are in a real conflict, but we hope that these words will be in their minds, helping to guide their actions as they put the Conflict CAT into their own words.*

Role play should show all the parts of the Conflict CAT. Here are the steps:

1. Go up the Conflict Escalator - ***briefly (10 seconds).***

2. One person says "We're going up the Conflict Escalator."

3. One person says "Let's breathe" or "Let's do Take Five Breathing."

4. Both people apologize for their role in escalating the conflict.

5. One person offers a solution based on one of the tools.

Rules: No touching each other, no inappropriate language, keep the part where you are going up the Conflict Escalator very brief - 10 seconds or so.

Give each pair one of these conflict scenarios:

- You both want to be first in line.

- You disagree about who has the coolest shoes.

- You are working on a school project together and you have different ideas of what it should be about.

- There is only one slice of pizza left and you both want it.

Share

Give some of the pairs a chance to share their role plays with the class. And have the class identify if they have included all of the steps of the Conflict CAT.

6. Alternative Activity

If you don't have enough time for the role plays or prefer not to do it, you can read the different conflict scenarios and talk through how you could use the Conflict CAT to work them out peacefully.

7. Closing

You might say: *Let's take a moment to think about something kind you could do for your Peace Partner today. You can close your eyes if you want to.* **Wait.**

Ask: *Who has an idea already of what you might do?* ***Take a few answers.***

Say: *Thanks for a great class, everyone!*

Ring a bell or chime if you have one.

Extensions: *See the Peace of Mind Core Curriculum for Middle School Unit 5, for 5 full lessons on Conflict Resolution, including the Conflict CAT. Page 110.*

Going up the Conflict Escalator?

The Conflict CAT Can Help!

Step 1: Calm Down

Imagine you are blowing out your birthday candles. Take a slow deep breath in and a slow deep breath out.

Step 2: Apologize

Take responsibility for whatever you did to make the conflict get bigger.

Step 3: Toolbox

Try one of these tools to work out a conflict peacefully:

Share
Take Turns
Compromise
Be Kind
Skip It
Flip a Coin
Pause the Conflict
Get Help

teachpeaceofmind.org

Lesson 10
Metacognition

<u>*Slides: 88-95*</u>

1. Introduction

You might say: *Today we are going to be learning about something called Metacognition. We're going to watch a video about Metacognition and today's new mindfulness practice is in the video. It's a different kind of mindfulness practice. Before we start that, let's have our Mindful Leader lead us in a mindful moment. Today the Mindful Leader can choose which practice we do.*

2. Mindful Moment

Choose the Mindful Leader

Have the Mindful Leader choose one of the practices the students have learned so far: Take Five Breathing, Gravity Hands, Blooming Breaths, or Four Square Breathing.

Watch What is Metacognition Video (3:55). This video includes mindfulness practice Counting Breaths and also teaches Remote Control breathing.

Discuss

- What is Metacognition?

- What is Remote Control Breathing?

- Was it difficult to keep your mind focused on counting your breaths?

- How do you think learning to notice what your mind is doing and to make decisions about what your mind is doing could be helpful to you?

- Is there something that you notice yourself thinking about all the time? Are you happy about this or is it something you would like to change?

- Does anybody want to share what channel your mind went to when you were trying to count your breaths?

3. American Sign Language (ASL)

You might say:*Today we're going to learn how to say "How are you feeling today?" in ASL. Then we'll be able to ask each other about how we are feeling and answer!*

You might say: *Let's watch a video of some Peace of Mind students showing us how to sign "How are you feeling today?."* **(the video is in the slides and here)**

ASL Practice: Have everyone try to say "How are you feeling today?" in ASL.

4. Peace Partners

Assign Peace Partners as in Lesson 1.

Peace Partners Activity: ASL Practice

You might say: *Try asking your Peace Partner how they are feeling today in ASL. Give them a chance to answer and then they can ask you and you can answer. If you have time go around and ask everybody in the class! The more you practice the easier it will get.*

Share with your Peace Partner a "channel" your mind goes to a lot when you are trying to do something else.

5. Whole Group Activity

Try the Count to Ten Game again.See Directions in Lesson 7.

You might say: *Today we are going to try the Count to Ten game again. This time try to notice what is happening in your mind while you are trying to concentrate and play the game.*

6. Closing

You might say*: Let's take a moment to think about something kind you could do for your Peace Partner today. You can close your eyes if you want to.*
Wait.
Ask*: Who has an idea already of what you might do?* **Take a few answers.**
Say*: Thanks for a great class, everyone!*
Ring a bell or chime if you have one.

Extension: *See the Peace of Mind Core Curriculum for Middle School, Unit 6 for additional lessons that explore applications of Remote Control Breathing including recognizing and responding to stereotypes and implicit bias.*

Lesson 11
The Negativity Bias

Slides: 96-103

1. Introduction

You might say: *Today we are going to learn about something called the Negativity Bias. It's something interesting that our brains do. Later we'll do an activity with our Peace Partner. But first let's do our mindful moment. I'm going to choose a Mindful Leader and ask them to choose what practice we will do today.*

2. Mindful Moment

Choose the Mindful Leader

Have the Mindful Leader choose and lead one of the practices the students have learned so far: Take Five Breathing, Gravity Hands, Blooming Breaths, or Four Square Breathing.

3. American Sign Language (ASL)

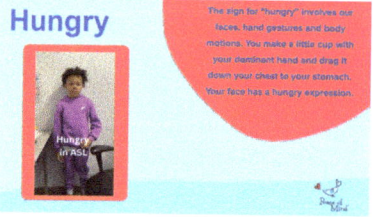

You might say: *Today we're going to learn how to say "hungry" in ASL. How do you feel in your body when you are hungry?*

Let's watch a video of some Peace of Mind students showing us how to sign "hungry." **(the video is in the slides and here)**

ASL Practice: Have everyone try to say "hungry" in ASL.

4. The Brain's Negativity Bias

Watch Negativity Bias video (8:27). The video contains a mindfulness practice and instructions for doing the Peace Partners Activity.

Discuss
- What is the Negativity Bias?
- Why does our brain do this strange thing?
- How does the Negativity Bias help us?
- How does the Negativity Bias hurt us?
- How can we hack the Negativity Bias?

5. Peace Partners

Assign Peace Partners as in Lesson 1.

Peace Partners Activity: Cups and Marbles

You might say: *Today we're going to do the activity that we learned in the video with our Peace Partners. I'm going to ask some volunteers to pass out the cups and marbles - each pair of Peace Partners gets 3 cups and a handful of marbles (or whatever small objects you have - paperclips, for example). One cup is the "Good" cup, one is the "Bad" cup, and the other cup is to hold the marbles.*

Directions (these are also in the video)

- Decide who will go first.
- The person who goes first will remember out loud everything about their day from the time they woke up. They will identify each thing as "good" or "bad".
- Students can decide what they want to share - it doesn't have to be everything.
- As the first person talks, their partner will put marbles in either the "good" or "bad" cup for each event **as directed by the sharer.**
- When you have reached the present moment, take a minute to notice: has the day been more good or bad so far?
- When the first person has finished, return the objects to their starting cup.
- The other person takes their turn.

> **Notes:** *Students may choose not to share every event in their day so far, and that is fine. As in all of these lessons, please respect students' decisions about how much to participate and share.*
>
> *It's important to remind kids that bad things sometimes happen and we're not trying to pretend that they don't. But our brains don't need help remembering those things. Our brains <u>do</u> need help remembering the good things, especially the little ones. So taming the Negativity Bias is a good way of helping us to see our lives as they really are - the good and the bad - and not just the bad.*

Discuss

Were you surprised by what you found?

- What were some of the good things you noticed?

- Did you notice that you had forgotten a lot of little good things?

- How did it feel to have your partner listening to you and putting marbles in the cup for you?

6. Closing

You might say: *Let's take a moment to think about something kind you could do for your Peace Partner today. You can close your eyes if you want to.*
Wait.

Ask: *Who has an idea already of what you might do?* **Take a few answers.**

Say: *Thanks for a great class, everyone!*

Ring a bell or chime if you have one.

Extension: *See the Peace of Mind Core Curriculum for Middle School, Unit 3, for two more lessons on Gratitude and the Negativity Bias.*

Sergio's Scale

Lesson 12
THINK Test Part I

Slides:104-110

1. Introduction

You might say: *Today we're going to be learning about mindful communication. We'll learn a new mindfulness practice and then I'm going to tell you who your Peace Partner is. We'll watch a second video on what happens when you say something you wish you hadn't. Whenever there are questions in the video, you are going to talk them over with your Peace Partner before sharing with the group.*

2. Mindful Moment

Watch Mindfulness Video Slow Breaths **with Rose (00:34).**

Choose the Mindful Leader
Have the Mindful Leader lead the Slow Breaths mindfulness practice as in the video.

3. American Sign Language (ASL)

You might say: *Today we're going to learn how to say "thirsty" in ASL. How do you feel in your body when you are thirsty?*

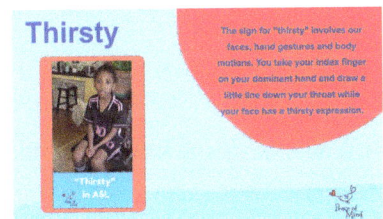

Let's watch a video of some Peace of Mind students showing us how to sign "thirsty" **(the video is in the slides and here)**

ASL Practice: Have everyone try to say "thirsty" in ASL.

4. Peace Partners

Assign Peace Partners as in Lesson 1.

Peace Partners Activity: Talk about the THINK Test

Watch video about the THiNK Test (6:44)

Stop the video at the following time stamps and give students a chance to talk with their Peace Partners about their answers and then ask a few people to share with the group.

1:24	What does that quote mean to you?
3:23	Is it True?
4:01	Is it Helpful?
4:30	Is it Necessary?
4:47	Are needs and wants the same?
5:13	Is it Kind?
5:37	What could Jared say instead?

Discuss

- So what do the letters THNK stand for?

- What does the "I" stand for?

- Are there times when you always need to use the THiNK Test?

- Are there times when you definitely don't need to use the THiNK Test?

- Can you think of a time when you wished you had used the THiNK Test?

5. Closing

You might say: *Let's take a moment to think about something kind you could do for your Peace Partner today. You can close your eyes if you want to.* **Wait.**
Ask: *Who has an idea already of what you might do?* ***Take a few answers.***
Say: *Thanks for a great class, everyone!*
Ring a bell or chime if you have one.

Extension: Please see the Peace of Mind Core Curriculum for Middle School, Lesson 4 on Mindful Communication, page 45.

Lesson 13
THiNK Test Part 2

<u>*Slides: 111-119*</u>

1. Introduction

You might say: *Today we're going to practice using the THiNK Test that we learned last time. We're going to imagine ourselves in different situations and let the THiNK Test help us speak mindfully. But first let's have our mindful moment.*

2. Mindful Moment

Choose the Mindful Leader

Have the Mindful Leader choose and lead one of the practices the students have learned so far: Take Five Breathing, Gravity Hands, Blooming Breaths, Four Square Breathing or Slow Breaths.

3. American Sign Language (ASL)

You might say: *Today we're going to learn how to say "peaceful" in ASL. Let's watch a video of some Peace of Mind students showing us how to sign "peaceful"* **(the video is in the slides and** <u>here</u>**)**

ASL Practice: Have everyone try to say "peaceful" in ASL.

4. Mindful Speaking

<u>**Watch the THiNK** Test Activity video</u> (6:00; start at 00:57) to see how this activity works.

Do the THiNK Test Activity

Choose 4 students to "be" the THiNK Test as in the video. Choose a fifth student to ask the questions. Choose a new group to be the THiNK Test for each question.

Choose from among these questions or create your own:

- I want to tell someone in my choir that their voice is bad.

- I want to tell everyone that I got 100% on the test .

- I want to tell someone that I just heard that "Ellen" likes "Fred."

- I want to tell someone that the TV show they like is for babies.

- I want to tell someone that their favorite YouTuber is inappropriate.

- Someone is spreading a rumor that I like "Ernie" and I want to set the record straight that I don't like him.

5. Peace Partners

Assign Peace Partners as in Lesson 1.

Peace Partner Activity: Two Truths and a Lie

You might say: *When I say "go!" you're going to find your Peace Partner and then you'll have a few minutes to play Two Truths and a Lie. You and your partner will take turns telling two truths about yourselves and one lie. Your partner has to guess what is true and what isn't true about you.*

6. Closing

You might say: *Let's take a moment to think about something kind you could do for your Peace Partner today. You can close your eyes if you want to.* **Wait.**
Ask: *Who has an idea already of what you might do?* Take a few answers.
Say: *Thanks for a great class, everyone!*
Ring a bell or chime if you have one.

Lesson 14
Just Like Me

<u>*Slides: 120-128*</u>

1. Introduction

You might say: *Today we're going to talk about compassion. We're going to learn two new compassion practices a little later in the lesson. First, I'll choose a Mindful Leader and ask them to lead us in a quick mindful moment of their choosing.*

2. Mindful Moment

Choose the Mindful Leader

Have the Mindful Leader choose and lead one of the practices learned so far: Take Five Breathing, Gravity Hands, Blooming Breaths, Four Square Breathing or Slow Breaths.

Watch Just Like Me Video (6:23) In this video students will learn two compassion practices: Heartfulness and Just Like Me. They'll get a chance to practice them both.

Stop the video at 4:03 to ask:
- What is compassion?
- What was it like for you to do the Heartfulness practice experiment?
- Did you notice any difference between thinning kind thoughts about yourself and thinking kind thoughts about others?

At the end of the video ask:
- What did it feel like to think those thoughts about somebody in the class?
- What did it feel like to think those thoughts about yourself?
- Without naming names, does anybody want to share how Just Like Me made you feel about the other person?

3. American Sign Language (ASL)

You might say: *Today we're going to learn how to say "worried" in ASL. How do you feel in your body when you feel worried?*

Choose a few volunteers to demonstrate what "worried" looks like.

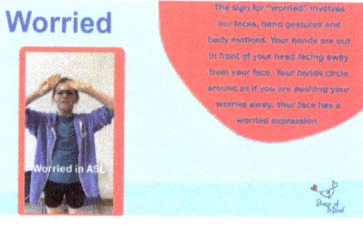

Let's watch a video of one of the Peace of Mind students showing us how to sign "worried" **(the video is in the slides and here)**

ASL Practice: Have everyone try to say "worried" in ASL. Point out that the sign involves our faces, hand gestures and body motions. Ask them if the sign matches the way that they feel when they feel worried.

4. Whole Group Activity: Walk, Stop, Wiggle Sit.

See directions in Lesson 8

5. Peace Partners

Assign Peace Partners as in Lesson 1.

Peace Partner Activity: Would You Rather
You might say: *When I say "go!", you're going to find your new Peace Partner and play Would You Rather.*

Write these questions on the board and/or read them aloud.
- Would you rather keep your first name or change it?
- Would you rather be able to read minds or to move things with your mind?
- Would you rather explore space or the ocean?
- Would you rather have x-ray vision or magnified hearing?
- Would you rather be stranded on an island alone or with someone who never stops talking?
- Would you rather be too hot or too cold?

6. Share out

Give everyone a chance to share one of their answers **and** one of their Peace Partner's answers.

7. Closing

You might say: *Let's take a moment to think about something kind you could do for your Peace Partner today. You can close your eyes if you want to.*

Wait.

Ask*: Who has an idea already of what you might do?* **Take a few answers.**

Say*: Thanks for a great class, everyone!*

Ring a bell or chime if you have one.

Extension: *See the Peace of Mind Curriculum for Middle School Lesson 20, Compassion for Self and Other. Expand further with Lesson 7, Find Your Feelings, to focus on how physical feelings relate to emotions.*

Lesson 15
Closing Session - Mindful Snowstorm

Slides: 129-138

1. Introduction

You might say: _This is the last lesson of the session. Today we're going to review what we've learned and share some ways that we might use what we've learned in our real lives. Before we have our last mindful moment together, we're going to make it snow!_

2. Whole Group Activity: Mindful Snowstorm

Pass out several strips of scrap paper and a pencil to everyone.

You might say: _Today we're going to see how many mindfulness practices we can remember. I'm going to ask you to write down a mindfulness practice that you remember on a piece of paper - just one practice per piece of paper. Write down as many as you can._

Next you're going to take your papers and ball it up so that it looks like a snowball.

When I say "go" we're going to **gently** toss our snowballs in the air.

Then everyone is going to pick up a nearby snowball and we'll take turns trying to demonstrate the mindfulness practice written on the paper. If you don't know how to do it you can pass. If you want to demonstrate it with a partner you can pick somebody to do it with you.

Ready? Go!

Do 4-5 rounds of this and see what they have remembered. Give compliments on their ability to teach and lead mindfulness practices that they didn't know when we started.

3. American Sign Language (ASL)

You might say: *Today we're going to learn how to say "loved" in ASL. How do you feel in your body when you feel loved?*

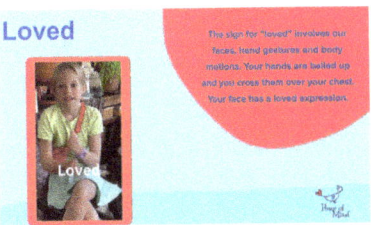

Choose a few volunteers to demonstrate what "loved" looks like.

You might say: *Let's watch a video of one of the Peace of Mind students showing us how to sign "loved".* **(the video is in the slides and here)**

ASL Practice: Have everyone try to say "loved" in ASL. Point out that the sign involves our faces, hand gestures and body motions. Ask them if the sign matches the way that they feel when they feel loved.

4. Group Activity: ASL Snowstorm

Pass out more slips of paper

You might say: *We have learned a lot in a short amount of time. Let's see what you remember and what you think you might use in your real life going forward. Write down one feelings word we learned in ASL. Just write one thing on each slip of paper. When you're done writing, turn your papers into snowballs.*

*When I say "go" we're going to **gently** toss our snowballs in the air again.*

Then everyone is going to pick up a nearby snowball and we'll take turns reading what is written on the papers and doing the ASL for each word.

5. Group Activity: Lesson Snowstorm

Pass out more slips of paper

You might say: *Now let's use our Hippocampus again to see what you remember. Write down one lesson or concept that you think you will use in your life - like the THiNK Test, or the Conflict CAT, or the brain science, etc. Just write one thing on each slip of paper. When you're done writing, turn your papers into snowballs.*

*When I say "go" we're going to **gently** toss our snowballs in the air again.*

Then everyone is going to pick up a nearby snowball and we'll take turns reading what is written on the papers and share our answers.

6. Peace Partners

Assign Peace Partners as in Lesson 1.

Peace Partner Activity: Teach it to a First Grader
You might say: *When I say "go," you'll find your Peace Partner and choose one of the lessons that you remember. Together you and your Peace Partner will think of a way to teach this lesson to a 1st grader. Is there a friend or family member you could teach it to?*

Share Ask for a couple of pairs of Peace Partners to share with the class.

7. Closing

This is our last class together. I hope that you enjoyed learning more about mindfulness, kindness, and how to work out our conflicts peacefully. The world needs lots of kind, mindful people. Now you have some tools to help you go out into the world and make it a more peaceful place. I hope you will!

Thank you so much!

About the Authors

Linda Ryden

Linda Ryden is the author of seven mindfulness-based children's books published by Cherry Lake Publishing and Peace of Mind Inc. Linda is the founder and Creative Director of Peace of Mind Inc. and creator of the Peace of Mind Program and author of the Peace of Mind Curriculum Series, a cutting-edge combination of mindfulness-based social-emotional learning, conflict resolution and social justice for Early Childhood through Middle School. Linda served as the full-time Peace Teacher at Lafayette Elementary School, Washington DC's largest public elementary school from 2003 to 2023, teaching Peace of Mind classes to more than 700 students every week.

Linda's work has been featured in The Washington Post, Washingtonian Magazine, Washington Parent, Washington Family, Teaching Tolerance, and Edutopia, among others. Linda was a keynote speaker at the National Network of State Teachers of the Year conference and a featured speaker at the National Education Association Foundation Symposium, and has received a Commendation for Educational Innovation from the DC Board of Education. Linda lives in Washington D.C. with her husband Jeremiah Cohen, owner of Bullfrog Bagels, and their dog Phoebe.

Ashley Brown

Ashley Brown is the Executive Director of Peace of Mind and a co-author of the *Peace of Mind Flex Curriculum*. She began her career as a classroom teacher, centering social-emotional learning and joy in both general education and inclusion settings as a high school English and special education teacher. Ashley holds a Master's degree in Counseling and has firsthand experience as both a teacher and a curriculum pilot, offering feedback on research-based ELA programs and their user design. At Peace of Mind, she brings her passion for student well-being and her expertise in program development, training, and implementation to help educators cultivate resilience, compassion, and conflict resolution skills in their classrooms and schools.

Bibliography

Bradshaw, C. P. (2015). Translating research to practice in bullying prevention. American Psychologist, 70 (4), 322-332.

Breeding, K., & Harrison, J. (2007). Connected and Respected: Lessons from the Resolving Conflict Creatively Program. Cambridge, Mass.: Educators for Social Responsibility.

Durlak, J. A., Weissberg, R. P., Dymnicki, A. B., Taylor, R. D. & Schellinger, K. B. (2011). The impact of enhancing students' social and emotional learning: A meta-analysis of school-based universal interventions. Child Development, 82(1): 405–432.

Hanson, R. (2015). Hardwiring Happiness. Random House USA.

Jennings, P. (2015). Mindfulness for teachers: Simple skills for peace and productivity in the classroom. The Norton Series on the Social Neuroscience of Education.

Jennings, P. A. (2019). The Trauma-Sensitive Classroom: Building Resilience with Compassionate Teaching. New York: W.W. Norton & Company.

Lantieri, Linda. "How SEL and Mindfulness Can Work Together." Greater Good. April 7, 2015. Accessed September 28, 2015. http://greatergood.berkeley.edu/article/item/how_social_emotional_learning_and_mindfulness_can_work_together.

Learning Heroes, Developing Life Skills in Children: A Road Map for Communicating with Parents, https://bealearninghero.org/parent-mindsets/ September 2018

O'Brennan, L., & Bradshaw, C. (2013). School Climate: A Research Brief. A report prepared for the National Education Association, Washington, DC.

Rechtschaffen, D., & Kabat-Zinn PhD, J. (2014). The Way of Mindful Education: Cultivating Well-being in Teachers and Students. Norton Books in Education. Schonert-Reichl, K. A., & Lawlor, M. S. (2010). The effects of a mindfulness-based education program on pre-and early adolescents' well-being and social and emotional competence. Mindfulness, 1(3), 137-151.

Schonert-Reichl, K. A., Oberle, E., Lawlor, M. S., Abbott, D., Thomson, K., Oberlander, T. F., & Diamond, A. (2015). Enhancing cognitive and social–emotional development through a simple-to-administer mindfulness-based school program for elementary school children: A randomized controlled trial. Developmental Psychology, 51(1), 52-66.

Seppala, E., Simon-Thomas, E., Brown, S. L., Worline, M. C., Cameron, C. D., & Doty, J. R. (2017). The Oxford Handbook of Compassion Science. New York, NY: Oxford University Press.

Siegel, D. J., & Bryson, T. P. (2012). The Whole-Brain Child. London: Constable & Robinson.

Simmons, Dena (2019), Why We Can't Afford Whitewashed Social-Emotional Learning Retrieved from http://www.ascd.org/publications/newsletters/education_update/apr19/vol61/num04

Srinivasan, M. (2014). Teach, Breathe, Learn: Mindfulness in and out of the Classroom. Berkeley, CA: Parallax Press.

Treleaven, David (2018). Trauma-Sensitive Mindfulness: Practices for Safe and Transformative Healing. New York: W. W. Norton & Company.

Weare, K. (2013). Developing mindfulness with children and young people: A review of the evidence and policy context. Journal of Children's Services, 8(2), 141-153.

Zoogman, S., Goldberg, S.B., Hoyt, W.T., & Miller, L. (2015). Mindfulness interventions with youth: A meta-analysis. Mindfulness, 6, 290 - 302.

Zenner, C., Hermleben-Kurz, S., & Walach, H. (2014). Mindfulness-based interventions in schools: A systematic review and meta-analysis. Frontiers in Psychology, 5, article 603.

Appreciation

Peace of Mind is based in our community, and we are so lucky to have the support and guidance and help of so many wonderful people. We are grateful to Mike Di Marco, Valentina Gabrielli and the teachers and staff of Horizons Greater Washington for inspiring us to create this curriculum and being our first pilot program in summer 2024. A fantastic group of educators in the DC area and beyond piloted the Flex Curriculum during the 24-25 school year and provided helpful feedback. This curriculum wouldn't exist without many wonderful friends of Peace of Mind including Kelly Gilstrap, Jillian Diesner, Jodi Ferrier, Elie Goldman, Jennifer Greene, our friends at Metamer Studios, and the students who helped to create the amazing ASL and mindfulness videos. As always, we are able to do what we do at Peace of Mind thanks to the support of very generous foundations and kind individual donors! Thank you!!